For You
and your amazing brain.
Because together
you are magnificent.

Dear You love from your Brain

Karen Young
Illustrated by Norvile Dovidonyte

Hey Sigmund
PUBLISHING

Dear You,

I love being in your head because it's magnificent and the sound of your voice is adorable from here! You and I are going to be best buds forever. The more you understand about me, the more you can help me be the best brain for you.

I'm kind of complicated, but fabulous. I'm made up of over 86 billion tiny building blocks called 'neurons', which are brain cells. If you were to count them one by one, it would take over three thousand years. It would also take a lot of patience and a distraction-free zone because it would be terrible to lose count at, like, 85 billion.

Brains can change and strengthen – and guess who can make that happen. You, Superstar! It's you! Let's talk about how.

You are a brain builder!

There are lots of different parts to me – parts for thinking, feeling, remembering, learning, and so much more. To be the best brain I can be, I need strong connections between the neurons **inside the parts** (so they are strong) and **between the parts** (so they work well together). Here's how this happens ...

Whenever you do something, the neurons involved in that action connect to form a pathway. Messages travel along this pathway with information for your brain and body about what to do.

Every time you repeat that action, the messages travel along the same pathway. The more this happens, the stronger the connections between the neurons get, and the stronger the pathway gets.

When a pathway gets super strong, the messages travel quicker along that pathway, and the action becomes easier or more 'automatic'.

This is how you become good at things - and trust me, Superstar, you can become good at so many things!

Neurotransmitters. Your special messengers.

Neurons don't touch. They love each other, so it's not about that. They just like their space, so they have teeny gaps between them. Messages are carried across those teeny gaps, from neuron to neuron, by special messengers called **neurotransmitters.**

Neurotransmitters love it when there are lots of them. When your neurotransmitters are at healthy levels, you'll learn better, sleep better, and feel calmer and happier.

Exercise, sleep, mindfulness, and eating well are excellent ways to keep your neurotransmitters at healthy levels.

How to learn new things and get better at what you do.

You have plenty of neurons waiting to connect into pathways.

If you want to learn something, start doing it.

If you want to get better at something, keep doing it.

Most importantly, never give up.
Strong pathways take time to build, so keep going.

You're going to love you for it. Promise.

But learning new things can be hard!

New things can feel clumsy at first because the pathways still need to strengthen. Every time you do that new thing, the pathway gets stronger.

Here's an example. When you first ride a bike, you'll wobble because the 'riding a bike' pathway isn't built yet. The more you ride, the stronger the pathway gets, and the more you become a legend on a bike.

Just keep doing the things you want to be good at and leave the rest to me. I've got you, Superstar!

Strong pathways can be excellent - or not.

Strong pathways are built by whatever you do most, whether those things are good for you or not. Let me explain.

If you keep choosing screen time over other things, the 'I need screen time' pathway will strengthen. Eventually, screen time will start to become easier and more automatic. This is how habits happen – the good ones and the not so good ones.

Thoughts also create pathways.
The more you think a thought, the more real it will feel.

If you keep thinking, **'I can't do hard things,'** it will start to feel like a truth. This will have nothing to do with how capable you actually are, and everything to do with a strong thought pathway.

If you keep thinking, **'I love that I give things a go,'** or, **'I'm one of the best people I've met since breakfast!'** you'll love yourself more and more. (And so you should! Have you met yourself, Bud? I've met you and I love you more than popcorn!)

Potato
CHIPS

While we're talking about thoughts ...

Thoughts can influence how you feel. Let me show you.

Think of something lovely. Maybe a special place, or someone you love to be with. (Awww, are you thinking of you? Me too!)

Now think of swimming in a freezing cold lake, or cuddling a furry rabbit, or eating ice-cream. How does your body change when you think of different things? How do your feelings change?

Sometimes thoughts get sticky and stay for a while. Some will make you feel good, and some will make you feel more 'ugh'. Thoughts aren't good or bad. They're just thoughts.

Let them come, then let them go.

Don't let those thoughts tell you that the only way they'll go is if you give them a cuddle and drop them at a bus stop. Honestly Superstar, you won't need to do any of that. Mindfulness, talking about it, or shifting your focus to other thoughts or activities will help move them on too.

Gratitude helps build stronger 'feel good' thought pathways. Each night, think of 3 things you're grateful for, or 3 things you love, or 3 things you've done well - or one of each!

You know what I love?
You, and these four dazzlers ...

Get your body moving.

If I could, I'd wear leggings and exercise all the time – but I'm not that into pants and it's squishy up here, so it's over to you. Walk, run, kick a ball, dance, go hula hooping – anything that gets your body moving.

When you exercise, I get stronger!

Eat well.

Being a brain is busy work, so I need you to fuel me up. Salmon, green leafy vegetables, and berries are some of my faves.

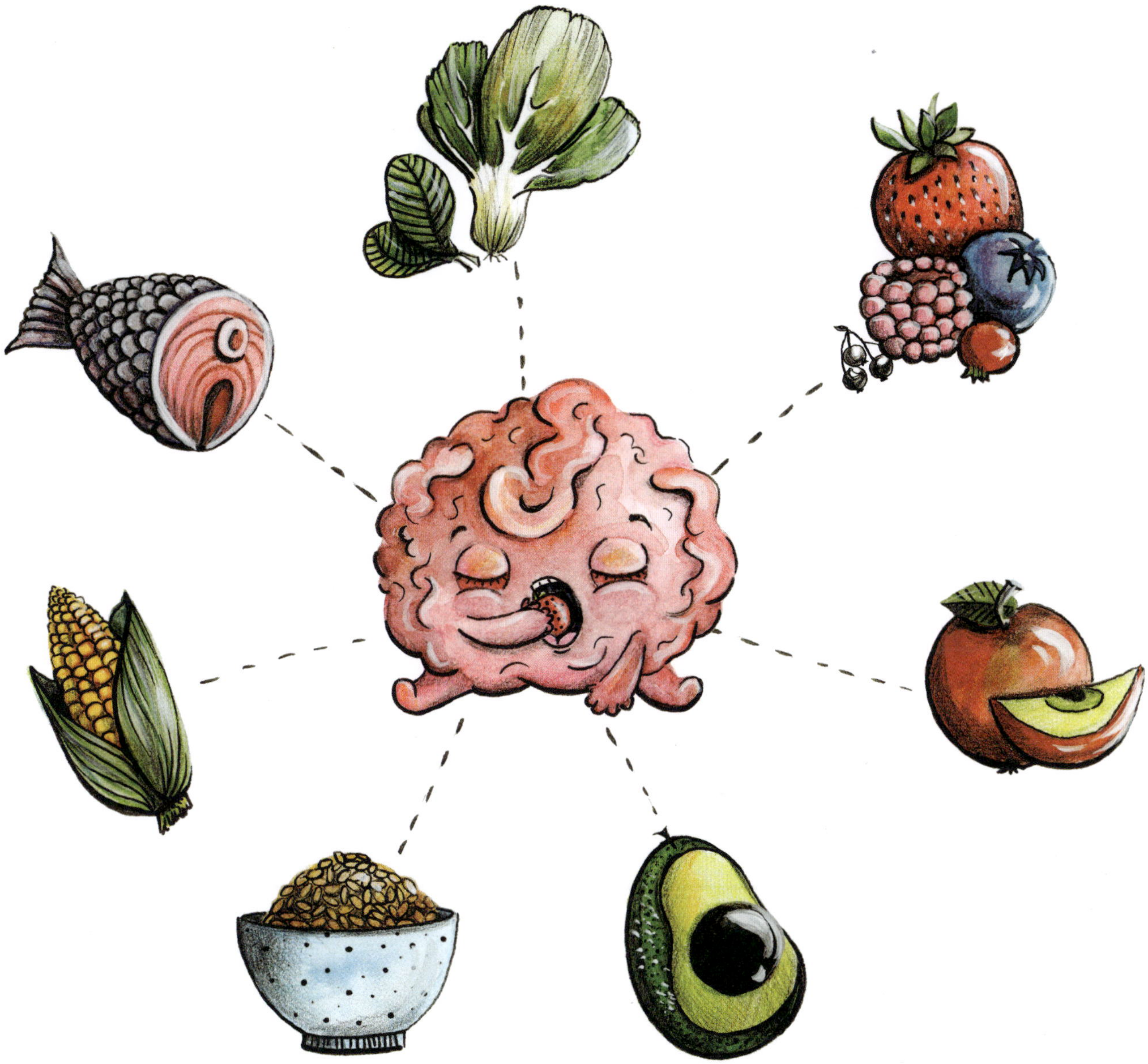

Wait. What? Don't scrunch your face! If a food tastes disgusting, it's because the 'this tastes okay' pathway isn't there yet. Keep trying teeny bits. If it's gross, start by licking it. (But don't lick juicy lemons. If a lemon needs licking, ask someone else to do it. Okay?)

Mindfulness

Mindfulness is exercise for brains. I love it. It makes me stronger so I can help you sleep better, learn better, and feel happier. Being mindful means focusing on one thing at a time. This might be your breathing, sounds, smells, the water when you shower – anything.
Start with a few minutes every day and work up from there.

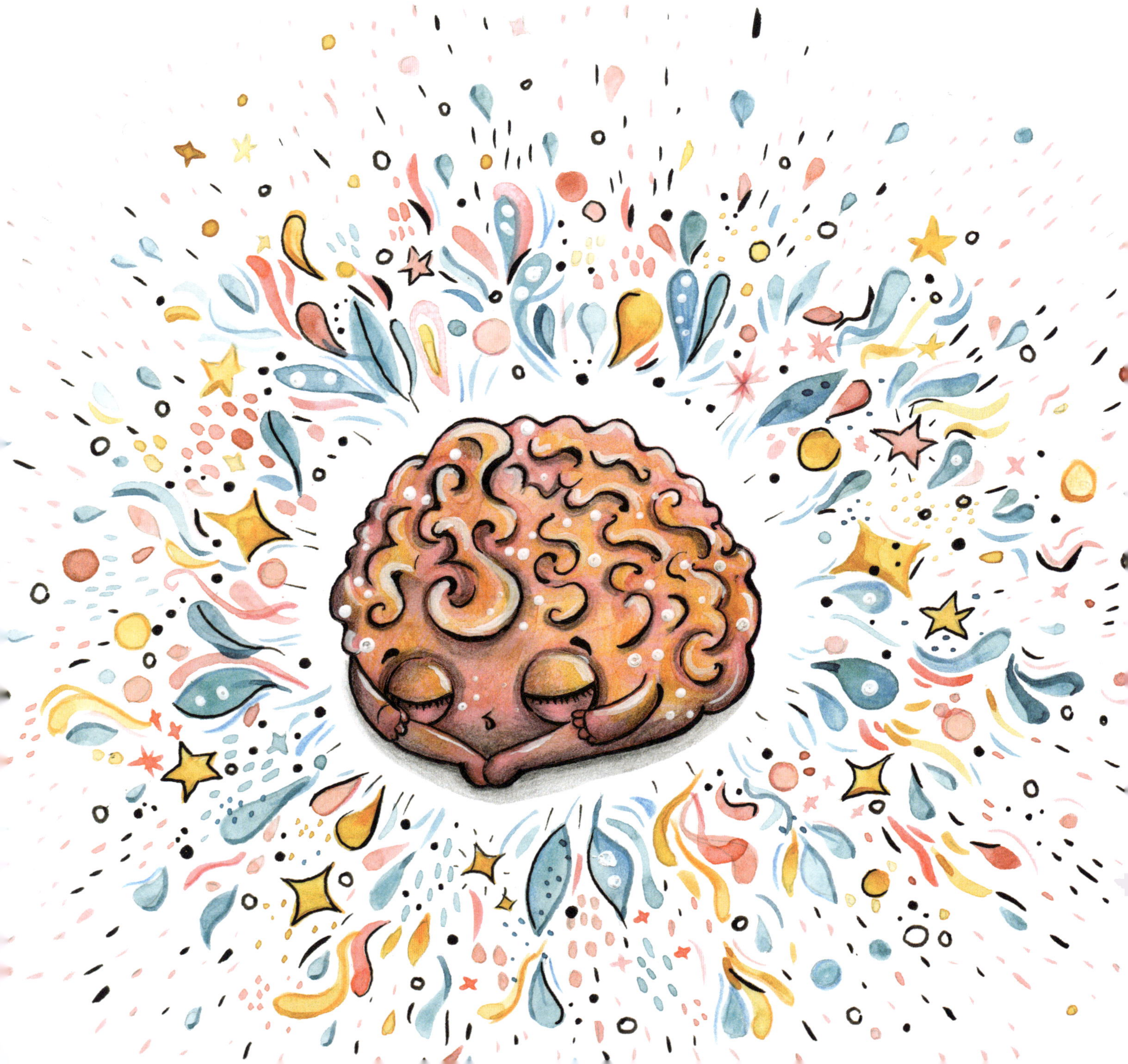

Sleep

I do so much while you're asleep!
I strengthen your learning and memories, help you feel better about things that have upset you, and clean up in here. I can also get creative and solve problems because I'm not busy with your 'awake' jobs, like talking, walking, and remembering not to lick lemons.

Brains are smart, and yours is magnificent, but all brains read things wrong sometimes.

I love you, and I want to keep you safe. And alive.
Brains love keeping people alive. We adore it actually.

There is a special part of me that works hard to keep you safe.
It's called the **amygdala** and it's like your own protective warrior.

When your amygdala thinks there might be trouble, it surges your body with a super body fuel to make you stronger, faster, and more able to fight the danger or run from it.

Your amygdala is brilliant, but it can get dramatic at times and fuel you up to deal with 'danger', even though you're safe. (Everyone's amygdala does this sometimes!)

When this happens, you might get a racy heart, clammy skin, sick tummy, and tight or wobbly muscles. This is anxiety. It can feel awful but it's completely safe.

You were built for brave things.

A strong, protective amygdala might read all sorts of things as danger, including anything that comes with a chance of making a mistake, being humiliated, or being away from someone you care about. This is why brave, important things, like trying something new or facing a challenge, might feel scary sometimes. That's why they're brave!

Your amygdala won't always know the difference between **scary and safe**, and **scary and dangerous**, which is why you need to be the boss.

When you feel anxious, ask yourself,
Do I feel like this because of a real threat, or because there is something important I need to do?
Then ask,
Is this a time to be safe (sometimes it will be), or is this a time to be brave?

The secret to being brave is knowing that you can **feel** anxious and **do** brave, even if it's just one tiny step at a time.
When something feels big, ask yourself,
What's one teeny step that would be braver than last time?
What can I do that would be brave right now?

I have a thinking part and a feeling part.

The thinking part is at the front.

It helps you think things through, solve problems, learn, make good decisions, and calm big feelings (and your amygdala). Let's call it the 'thinking brain'.

The feeling part is behind it.

It helps you feel your feels, stay safe, and love your people. Your amygdala lives here. Let's call it the 'feeling brain'.

They work best as a team.

When they work together, the feeling brain will let you know when something doesn't feel right, and the thinking brain will help you respond well.

Mindfulness strengthens your thinking brain, your feeling brain, and the pathway between the two (so they can work as a team).

All feelings matter.

Feelings have important jobs to do, even the ones that aren't lovely to feel. They move you to ask for help, love your people, care about things, and change things that need changing.

Sometimes when feelings get big, you might do things that aren't so adorable. Maybe you're thinking, **'Yes. This might have happened once or hundreds of times, but only when there's been a very good reason.'**

Oh, I hear you, Superstar! The reason will always be important, but so is letting those feelings happen safely, without hurting anyone or landing you in trouble.

This isn't always easy. When feelings get big, the amygdala tries to switch off the thinking brain for a while. This makes it easier to act fast because your thinking brain isn't taking time to, you know, think. This can help you get to safety quickly, but it makes it harder to do important thinking brain things, like making good decisions about what to do or say.

Let's talk about how to bring your thinking brain back into action.

How to calm your amygdala and bring your thinking brain back.

Breathe ... In. Out. Lovely.

Strong, steady, breathing is like a lullaby for your amygdala. Try to do a few minutes each day when you're calm. This will strengthen the 'strong, steady breathing' pathway so it will be easier to do when your feelings get big.

Talk about it.

I have a right side and a left side. They also need to work as a team. The left side loves language and helping you think clearly. The right side loves feelings. During big feelings, the right side tends to take over. Talking or writing (left side specialty) about how you're feeling (right side specialty) helps them come back together as a team.

Use your finger to draw a sideways figure 8 on your skin.
As you draw the first loop, breathe in for 3, hold in the middle for 1, then breathe out for 3 on the second loop. Do this for a minute or two.

More ways to calm your feeling brain, switch on your thinking brain, and strengthen the 'teamwork' pathway between the two.

Walk, swing, sway, dance.

Brains love rhythm and movement. It helps us feel calm and safe.

Listen to music.

Because sweet, sweet rhythm. I love rhythm so much that if I wasn't a brain, I probably would have been a dancer. Or a drummer. But I love being your brain more than anything.

Count slowly to 10 or backwards from 10.

Counting switches your thinking brain on. You can't count without it!

Blow some power bubbles.

Take a strong steady breath and let a thought come to you. Put it inside an imaginary bubble and watch it float around in front of you for a while. When you're ready, gently blow the bubble away and let your thought float away with it. Keep going for as long as you like.

Imagine calming your amygdala.

What are the words it needs to hear to know you're okay? Maybe something like, **'I'm okay. I've got this.'** Now, say those words to yourself and feel the calm happen.

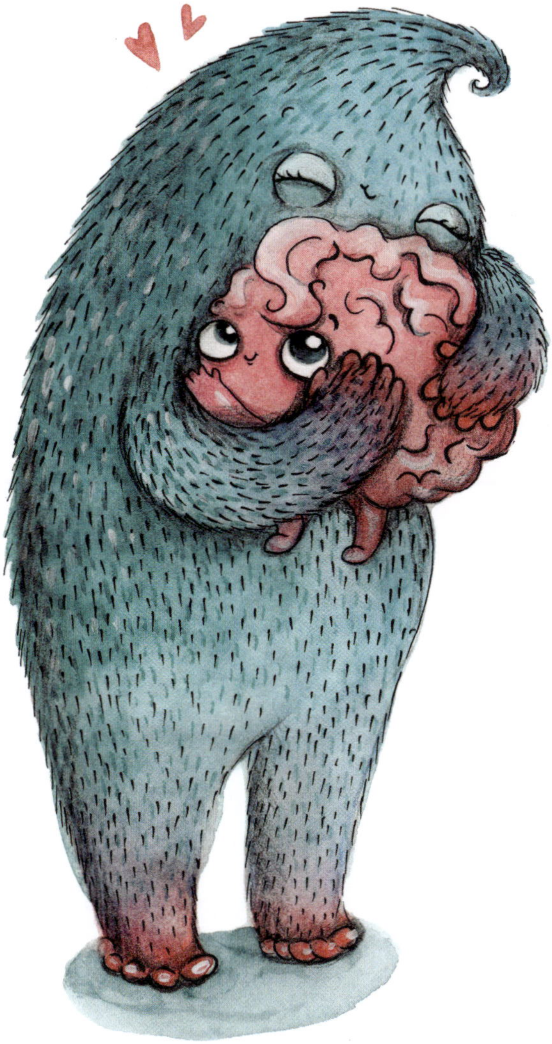

Think of your brain like a muscle.

Every time you use your thinking brain to do thinking brain things, it will strengthen. The stronger your thinking brain is, the more it will be able to stay on when your amygdala tries to switch it off. This will let you feel your feels and be smart about it.

Let's talk about 'feel goods'.

A neurotransmitter called **dopamine** is released when you do things that feel good for you. Its job is to make you want to do more of those things.

Some good things that release dopamine are trying new things, being with people who feel good to be around, exercising, eating good food, and succeeding at a challenge.

But be careful, Superstar ...

Dopamine can be a sneaky little trickster. It can make you want 'more' when 'more' is not a good idea. Gaming, screen time, and sugary snacks can also release dopamine. A little of these is lovely, but too much of anything is too much.

Remember, just because it feels good, doesn't mean it's good for you.

Do the things that make you happy but check in with your thinking brain along the way. Two sweets are great. Five might be okay. More than that might have your thinking brain saying, 'Ooohhh, Bud – I tried to tell you ... You should have stopped after four. Maybe five. But seventeen?! Bud! How do we explain this to your belly?! Just tell it you love it, and you'll send down some berries when it feels better.'

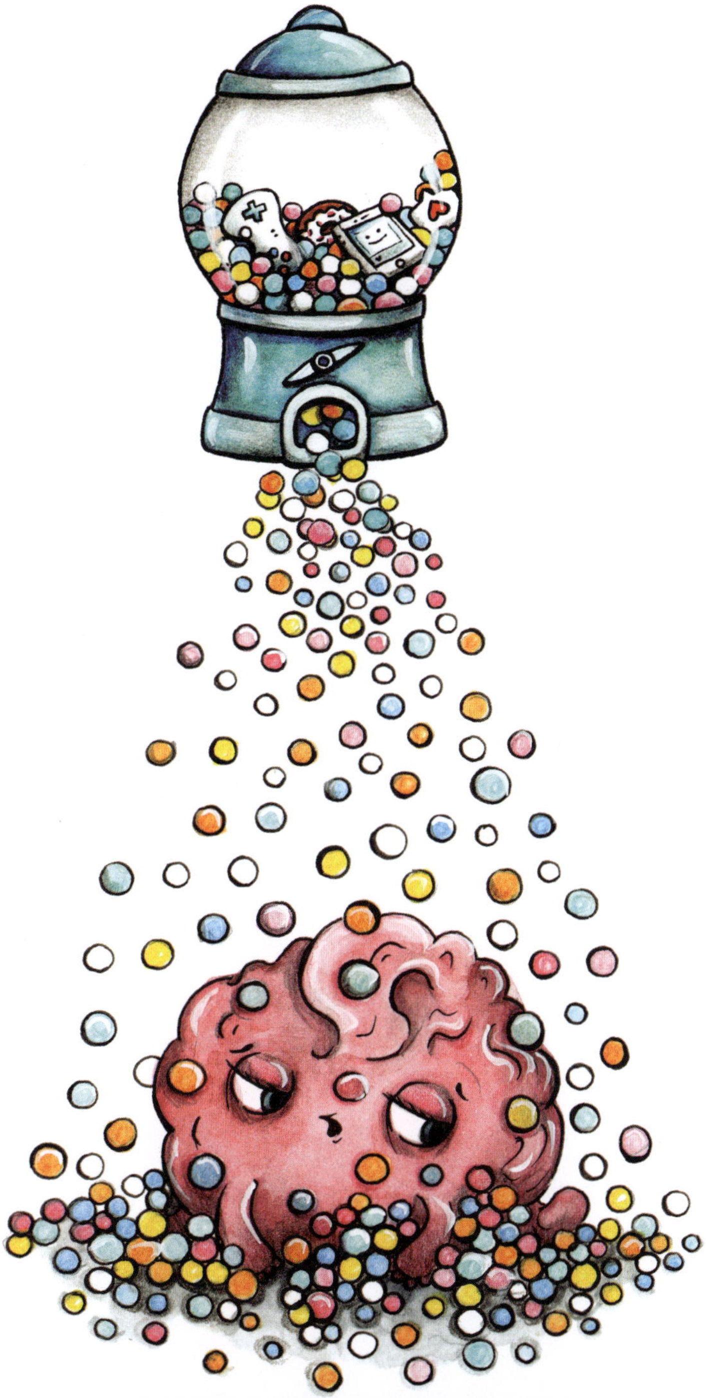

We're the same, but different - and that's a great thing!

Every brain is different, and all brains are awesome. Different experiences build different pathways, which build different brains. There is nobody else like you, but everyone is the same as you in some ways and different to you in others. The more you cherish the similarities and appreciate the differences, the more pathways you'll build around being kinder and wiser.

(And just when I thought you couldn't be any more adorable, there you'll go, being more adorable!)

It's cool to be kind.

Kindness is a superpower. Write it on your mirror and tell the others. Whenever you do something kind I want to squeal with pride. I don't though, because, you know ... headaches. Instead, I release dopamine and other 'feel good' chemicals. When you do good, you feel good. I'm here to make sure.

Always remember,

If there are three things the world will always need a lot of,
it's you, sunshine, and more people as amazing as you.

There's so much to learn and see and feel and do, but there's no hurry.
Stay curious, kind, and brave, and we'll just keep getting stronger.
Don't worry if you make mistakes along the way.
Mistakes are how brains learn and strengthen.

Being your brain is the best thing that's ever happened to me.
You are important and needed and the world will always be
better for having you in it. With all the people in the world
to be a brain for, I got the best one.

Love you, Superstar.
Thanks for believing in us.

About the Author

Karen Young

Karen began her career as a psychologist and now consults with parents, schools, government bodies, and child and adolescent focused organisations both at home in Australia and overseas. She is the founder of Hey Sigmund at www.heysigmund.com, an internationally popular online resource that provides contemporary, research-driven information on anxiety, parenting, and the neurodevelopment of children. She has written three books, including the bestselling 'Hey Warrior'.
The books have been translated into multiple languages and are used extensively in homes, schools, and therapeutic settings throughout the world.

About the Illustrator

Norvile Dovidonyte

Norvile graduated art school in Lithuania and got a bachelor degree of fine photography in Vilnius Design College. Ever since she can remember, she has been fascinated by children's storybooks, and especially creative illustrations. She lives with her photographer boyfriend who supports and inspires her every day. You can find her works at www.norvile.com.